Please check all items for damages
before leaving the Library.
Thereafter you will be held
responsible for all injuries
to items beyond reasonable wear.

Helen M. Plum Memorial Library

Lombard, Illinois

A daily fine will be charged for
overdue materials.

THE USBORNE BOOK OF
EASY
GUITAR
TUNES

Emma Danes

Designed by Paul Greenleaf

Original music and arrangements by
Caroline Hooper and Geoffrey Edge

Photographs by Howard Allman
Illustrated by Rian Hughes

Technical illustrations by Ross Watton

Guitar consultants: Geoffrey Edge
and Richard Buckton
Series editor: Anthony Marks

INTRODUCTION

This book contains lots of tunes in many different styles. You can play them on any type of guitar. As you go through the book, you will learn new notes, techniques, musical words and signs. The tunes get harder later in the book, so you may need to spend longer practicing them. Near the end there are tunes for more than one guitar. There are charts that show you how to play each note, and some common chords, on page 62. On page 63 there are tips about playing the pieces and a list of all the tunes in the book.

Tips on learning the tunes

1. Before you start to play a tune, work out any unfamiliar notes or rhythms.

2. Look for repeated left- or right-hand patterns in the music.

3. Try not to be discouraged by something which looks tricky. If you learn tunes slowly and carefully, they soon become easier.

4. Practice any difficult parts of the music a few times until you can play them well.

5. When you play, keep your eyes on the music not on the strings. With practice, both your hands will be able to find the correct notes and strings by themselves.

6. Keep your hands, arms, neck and shoulders relaxed as you play.

7. Play as often as you can, even if it is only for a short time.

Types of guitar

Electric, steel-string acoustic and classical guitars all have the same basic parts. The strings are wound around tuning keys at the head of the guitar and stretched over a bar called the nut. They run along the neck, go over the saddle and are attached to the bridge. The strings are numbered from the highest-sounding (first string) to the lowest-sounding (sixth string).

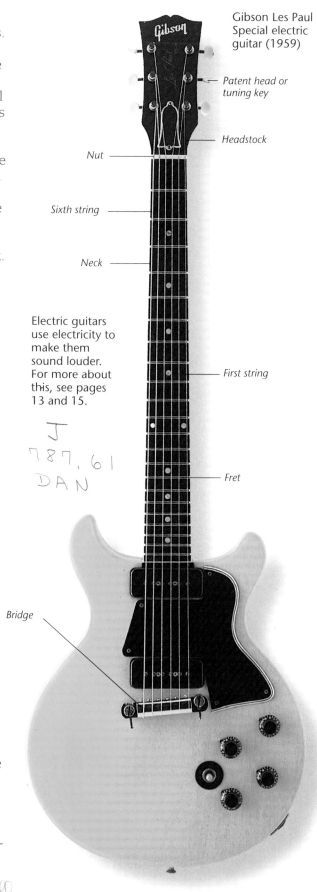

Gibson Les Paul Special electric guitar (1959)

Patent head or tuning key

Headstock

Nut

Sixth string

Neck

Electric guitars use electricity to make them sound louder. For more about this, see pages 13 and 15.

First string

Fret

Bridge

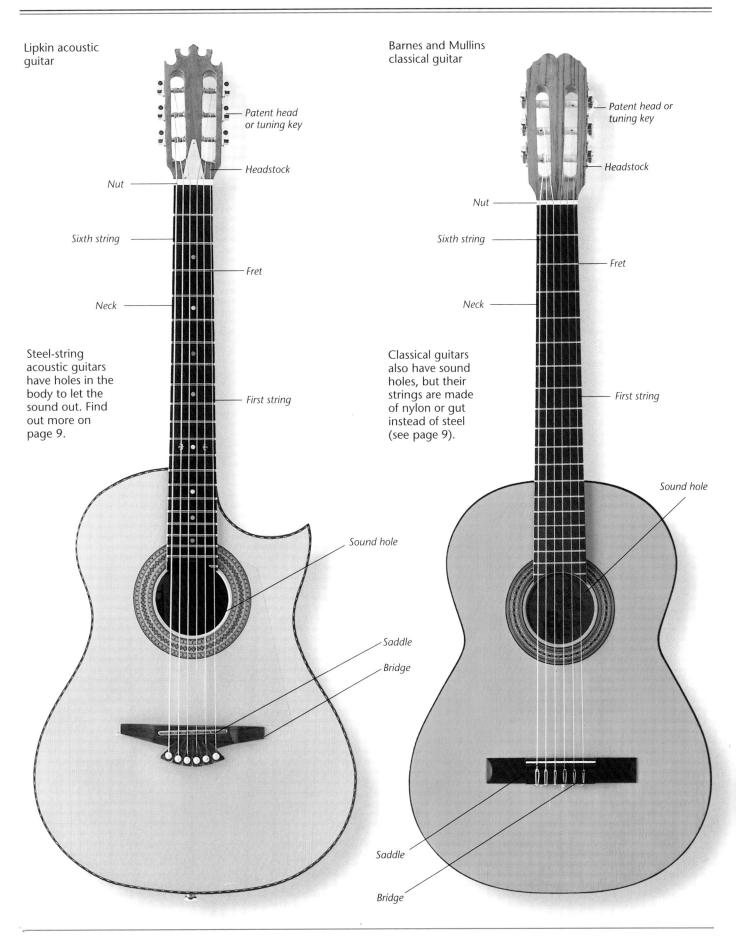

Lipkin acoustic
guitar

Barnes and Mullins
classical guitar

*Patent head
or tuning key*

Headstock

Nut

Sixth string

Fret

Neck

First string

Steel-string
acoustic guitars
have holes in the
body to let the
sound out. Find
out more on
page 9.

*Patent head or
tuning key*

Headstock

Nut

Sixth string

Fret

Neck

First string

Classical guitars
also have sound
holes, but their
strings are made
of nylon or gut
instead of steel
(see page 9).

Sound hole

Sound hole

Saddle

Bridge

Saddle

Bridge

STARTING TO PLAY

Getting comfortable

When you play the guitar, you must feel relaxed, so that your fingers are free to move easily. You can sit or stand to play an electric or steel-string acoustic guitar. Classical guitarists usually sit down, and hold the instrument in a special way.

Fender Stratocaster Deluxe (detail of Stratocaster neck on opposite page)

If you sit, rest the guitar on your right leg. Rest your arm on the side of the guitar. Don't let your wrist touch the body.

If you stand, use a guitar strap and adjust it so the guitar feels comfortable. Keep the neck as high as the body or a little higher.

To play a classical guitar, rest it on your left thigh and raise your leg a little. Lean forward a little if you need to see your hands.

How to play the strings

For the first few tunes in the book, play the strings with your right-hand first finger.

Alternatively you can use a small piece of plastic called a plectrum or pick.

Hold your wrist slightly arched and rest your thumb on the sixth string. Bend your finger and play the string with your fingertip.

Your finger pushes the string sideways. Finish with your finger above the strings, bent in towards the palm of your hand.

Hold a pick between your first finger and thumb, with your finger bent in a U-shape. Move your wrist to play the strings.

Left-hand position

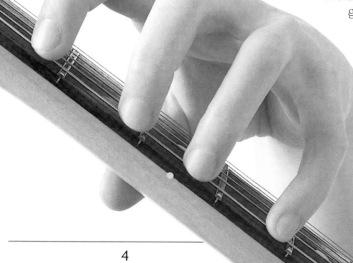

Hold your left thumb straight and place it on the back of the guitar neck, about in line with the second fret. Don't let the palm of your hand or the bottom of your fingers touch the neck. Curve your fingers over the strings so that when you press them down your fingertips are upright, at right angles to the strings. Your nails need to be fairly short to do this. Keep your hand and wrist relaxed.

Press the strings firmly just to the left of a fret. You should just be able to feel the fret. If you press too far from a fret the string will buzz. Don't press too hard, just firmly enough to make the note sound clear when you play it.

4

Tuning your guitar

Before you play, tune your strings so they play the correct notes. You do this by turning the tuning keys.

First, play your open sixth string (open means you do not press it with your left hand). Tune it to sound the same as a low E from a pitch pipe, tuning fork, electronic tuner or keyboard (on the keyboard below, low E is labeled "6th string note"). Next, you tune each string in turn, matching it to a note you play on the string below it. Follow the instructions below. The numbered dots in the picture on the left show you which notes to use.

① Play the note at the fifth fret of the sixth string. Tune your fifth string to this note.

② Play the note at the fifth fret of the fifth string. Tune your fourth string to this note.

③ Play the note at the fifth fret of the fourth string and tune your third string to it.

④ To hear the note to tune your second string to, play the note at the fourth (not fifth) fret of the third string.

⑤ Play the note at the fifth fret of the second string and tune the top string to it.

Finally check that the first and sixth strings sound like higher and lower versions of the same note.

If you find this tricky at first, you can get the notes from a piano or keyboard. Or you can use an electronic tuner.

4th fret

5th fret

Blow the E pipe next to the A pipe to hear the note for your sixth string.

You can use a tuning fork labeled E 329.6 Hz to hear the note for your sixth string.

Hit one of the prongs sharply on your knee to hear the note.

A dial on an electronic tuner tells you when each string is in tune.

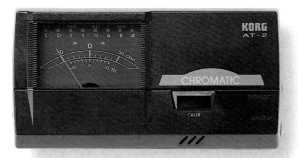

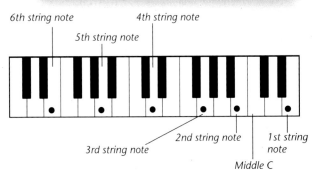

6th string note

5th string note

4th string note

3rd string note

2nd string note

1st string note

Middle C

READING MUSIC

Guild acoustic
(detail of Guild
neck below)

The tunes in this book are written on a set of five lines called a staff (or stave). The pitch is how high or low a note is. The higher the pitch, the higher up the staff it is. Some notes are too high or low to fit on the staff.

They have extra short lines above or below the staff. The pitch names go alphabetically from A to G, then start at A again. A sign called a treble clef at the start of the staff means that a note on the second line up is G.

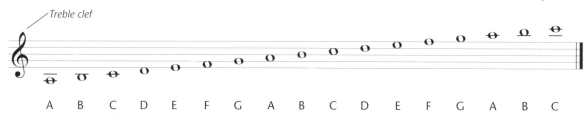

Treble clef

A B C D E F G A B C D E F G A B C

Finding the notes on your guitar

The picture below shows you how to play the notes in the first tune. A circle by the nut means the note is an open string (this means that you don't press a left-hand finger down).

A dot by a fret shows you where to press the string. Below you can see how the notes are written on a staff. Practice finding each note, then looking at it on the staff.

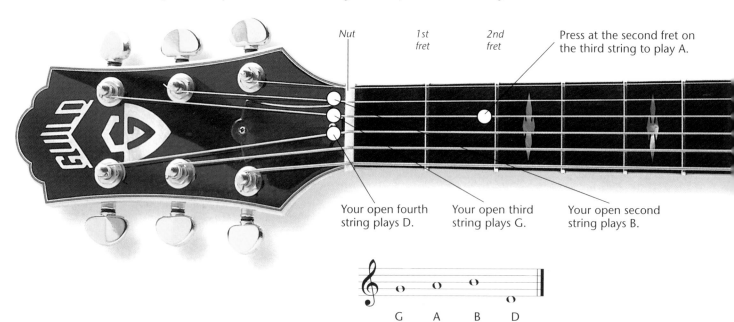

Nut

1st fret

2nd fret

Press at the second fret on the third string to play A.

Your open fourth string plays D.

Your open third string plays G.

Your open second string plays B.

G A B D

In this book, there is a diagram showing you how to play each new note. You will find these diagrams down the sides of the pages. You can see how the diagrams work below.

In the music, a number before each note tells you which finger to use (O means play an open string). A number in a circle below or on the staff tells you which string to press.

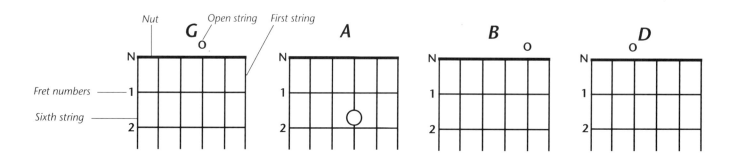

Nut   Open string   First string

G   *A*   *B*   *D*

Fret numbers — 1

Sixth string — 2

Counting

As you play, you have to count the length of each note in steady counts (called beats). You count the silences (called rests) too.

Below you can see the four most common types of notes and rests. Clap through the first few tunes before you try to play them.

A quarter note lasts for one beat.

A half note lasts for two quarter beats.

A whole note lasts for four quarter beats.

An eighth note lasts for half a quarter beat.

Two eighth notes joined

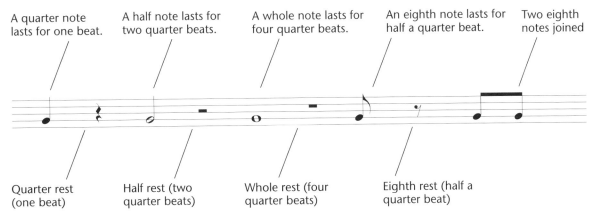

Quarter rest (one beat)

Half rest (two quarter beats)

Whole rest (four quarter beats)

Eighth rest (half a quarter beat)

Washburn EA20 acoustic

Time signatures

Beats are arranged in groups called measures. Numbers called the time signature at the beginning of a tune tell you how to count. The top number tells you how many beats are in each measure. The bottom number tells you what type of beats they are. 4 means they are quarter beats.

Four quarter beats in a measure.

Three quarter beats in a measure.

Walk, don't run

Now try playing this tune. First clap through the rhythm, then figure out all the notes.

When you play, count steadily and evenly so each note lasts for the right length of time.

Washburn D10NM acoustic

Five-bell chime

NEW NOTES

C

D

E

Au clair de la lune

Remember to look at the new note diagrams on the left.

Count 1   2   3   4   1 — 2   3 — 4   1   2   3   4   1 — 2 — 3 — 4

Left-hand fingers

When you play, keep your left-hand fingertips upright, at right angles to the strings. When you press your first finger down, keep your other fingers spread out a little, so they are ready to play. When you have pressed a finger down, don't lift it again until you have to. For example, in the first bar of *Au clair de la lune*, keep your first finger pressed down when you press your third finger down to play D. Then keep both fingers pressed down until the beginning of the third measure. Only take your third finger off when you have to play the C again.

Acoustic guitars

An acoustic guitar has a hollow body with an opening in it called a sound hole. When you play the strings, the air inside the guitar vibrates. The vibrations come out of the sound hole, and you hear them when they reach your ear. Most acoustic guitars have steel strings, but classical guitars always have nylon or gut strings. Never put steel strings on a classical guitar*.

An acoustic guitar taken apart

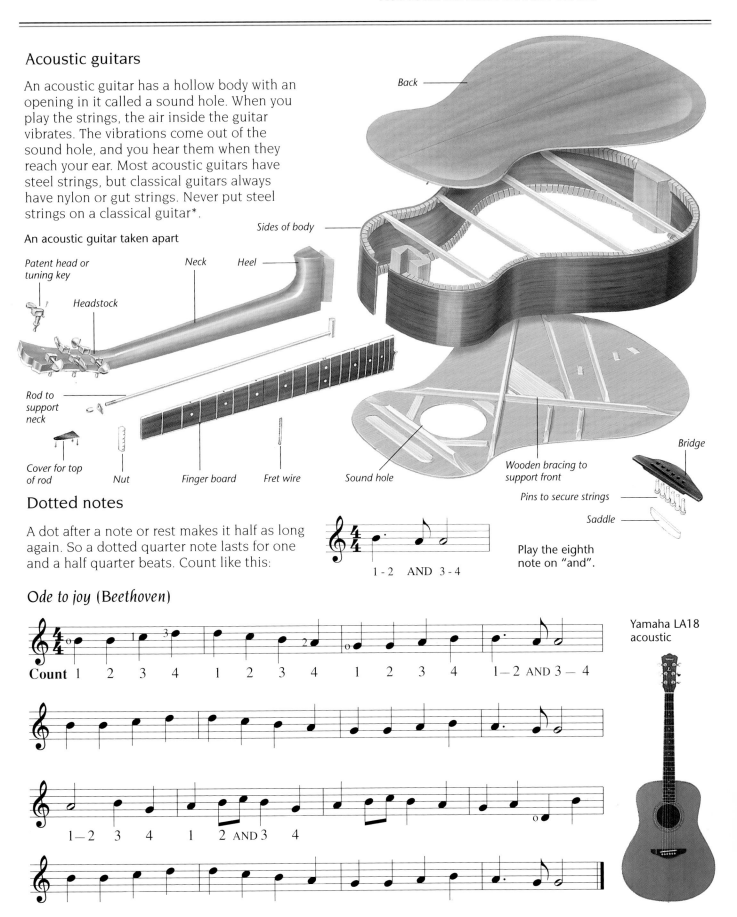

Back

Sides of body

Patent head or tuning key

Neck

Heel

Headstock

Rod to support neck

Cover for top of rod

Nut

Finger board

Fret wire

Sound hole

Wooden bracing to support front

Bridge

Pins to secure strings

Saddle

Dotted notes

A dot after a note or rest makes it half as long again. So a dotted quarter note lasts for one and a half quarter beats. Count like this:

1 - 2   AND   3 - 4

Play the eighth note on "and".

Ode to joy (Beethoven)

Count 1   2   3   4   1   2   3   4   1   2   3   4   1 — 2 AND 3 — 4

1 — 2   3   4   1   2 AND 3   4

Yamaha LA18 acoustic

USING YOUR RIGHT HAND

To play tunes smoothly and reach all the notes easily you have to play the strings with your right-hand thumb and first three fingers.

Look after your right-hand nails carefully. If they are ragged, the strings will not make a good sound when you play them. File them so that each nail curves slightly to the right.

Often you play notes on the bottom three strings with your thumb, and use your fingers for the top three strings.

Your right hand thumb and fingers are named after the first letter of the Spanish words for them.

Thumb: p
(pulgar)

Index finger: i
(indicio)

Middle finger: m
(medio)

Ring finger: a
(anular)

For the tunes in this book, you will not need your little finger.

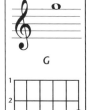

NEW NOTES

F

G

C

Playing with your thumb

Practice playing a string with your thumb. It should make a circle shape in the air. Make sure only your thumb moves, not your whole arm. The type of finger movement shown on the right and on page 4 is a called a free stroke. This is the most common stroke.

Hold your thumb straight. It makes a triangle with your fingers.

Push the string downward and outward. Finish above the string.

Minute minuet

In this tune, the letters *p*, *i*, *m* and *a* show you which right-hand finger to use for each string.

Follow the left-hand finger numbers carefully too, as they make the notes easier to play.

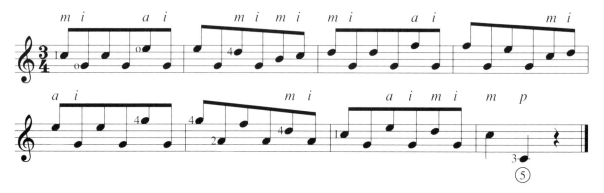

Moderato (Sor)*

Where there are several notes in a row on the same string, play them with different fingers.

A dotted half note lasts for a half note plus half a half note, or three quarter beats.

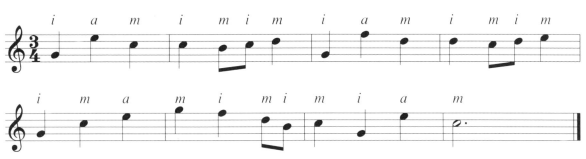

Andantino (Carulli)

Simon Ambridge classical guitar

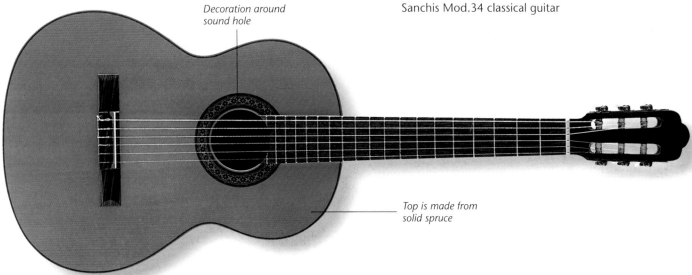

Decoration around sound hole

Sanchis Mod.34 classical guitar

Top is made from solid spruce

Ties

A tie is a curved line linking two notes of the same pitch. Play the first note for as long as both notes added together, instead of playing two separate notes.

1   AND - 2 - 3

Second note lasts for 2½ quarter beats

Steve Jones of the Sex Pistols, playing a Gibson Les Paul (see opposite page)

The house of the rising sun

Watch out for the tied notes and dotted half notes in this tune.

Open strings

When you play an open string before a rest or at the end of a tune, you have to touch the string to stop it from sounding for too long. The easiest way to do this is to damp the strings with the side of your right hand. After playing the note, don't move your fingers or thumb, but turn your whole hand over and gently bring it down so the side of your hand and thumb touch the strings.

Lavender's blue

Count three quarter beats on the last note, then damp the string.

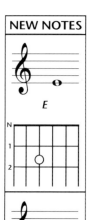

NEW NOTES

E

F

Electric guitars

Electric guitars can have a hollow or solid body, but the sounds have to be amplified electrically before you can hear them properly. Small microphones called pick-ups convert the string vibrations into electrical signals. These are sent to the amplifier and converted back into sounds, which come out of the loudspeaker.

A solid body electric guitar taken apart

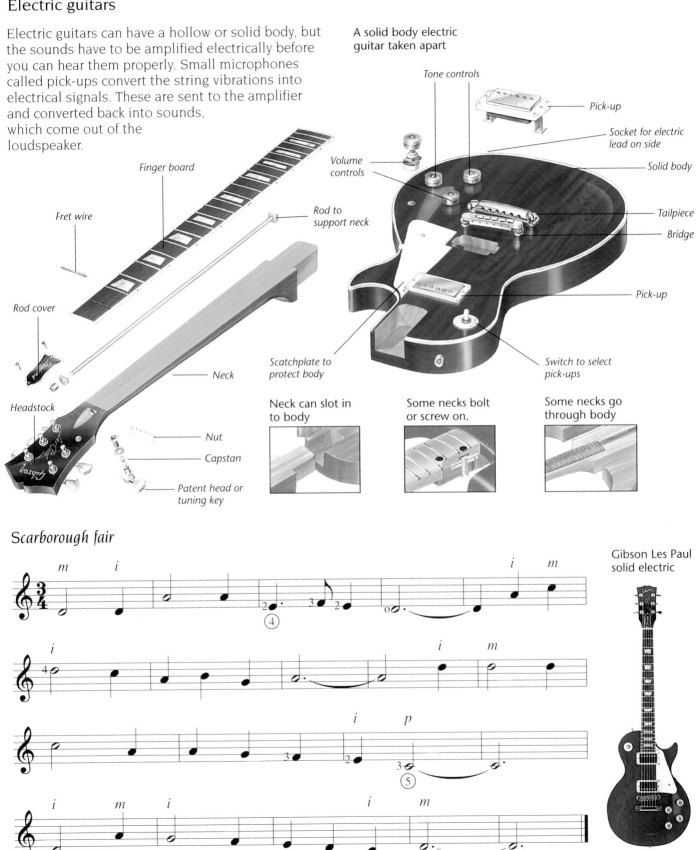

Finger board

Fret wire

Rod to support neck

Tone controls

Pick-up

Socket for electric lead on side

Volume controls

Solid body

Rod cover

Tailpiece

Bridge

Neck

Pick-up

Scatchplate to protect body

Switch to select pick-ups

Headstock

Nut

Capstan

Patent head or tuning key

Neck can slot in to body

Some necks bolt or screw on.

Some necks go through body

Scarborough fair

Gibson Les Paul solid electric

TUNES IN TWO PARTS

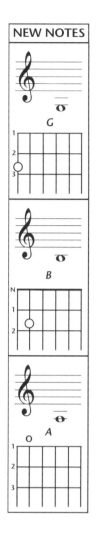

NEW NOTES

G

B

A

In most guitar music you play more than one note at a time. Usually there is a melody line printed with the stems of the notes going upward, a bass line, with the note stems downward, and often other notes between.

Your right thumb and fingers move past each other in a twisting movement as you play.

Keep each left-hand finger upright and pressed down until you need to move it to play another note.

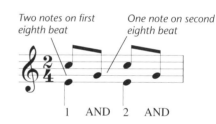

Melody note   *m*   *i*   *Right-hand fingering*

Left-hand fingering   *Bass-line note*

Start by learning each line separately, using the correct fingers on both hands. Then play both lines at once. Make sure that you play both notes at exactly the same time, so that they sound together. Also try to play the melody line a bit louder than the bass line.

Counting two part tunes

Often the melody and bass line of a tune have different rhythms. But each line always has the same number of beats in a measure. Count very carefully, thinking about which notes you have to play on each beat.

Two notes on first eighth beat   *One note on second eighth beat*

1   AND   2   AND

Play the second and fourth eighth notes on "and".

Study (Carulli)

Gibson ES350 electric acoustic (1962)

Allegretto (Giuliani)

Follow the left-hand fingering carefully in this tune.

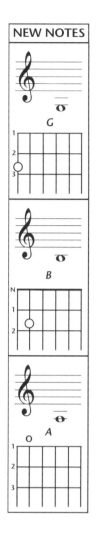

14

Electric acoustic guitars

Electric acoustic guitars have a hollow body as well as pick-ups. They have the same sound as an ordinary acoustic guitar, and can be heard without being amplified. But with electricity they can sound as loud as an electric guitar, and be used with special effects pedals (see pages 54-55).

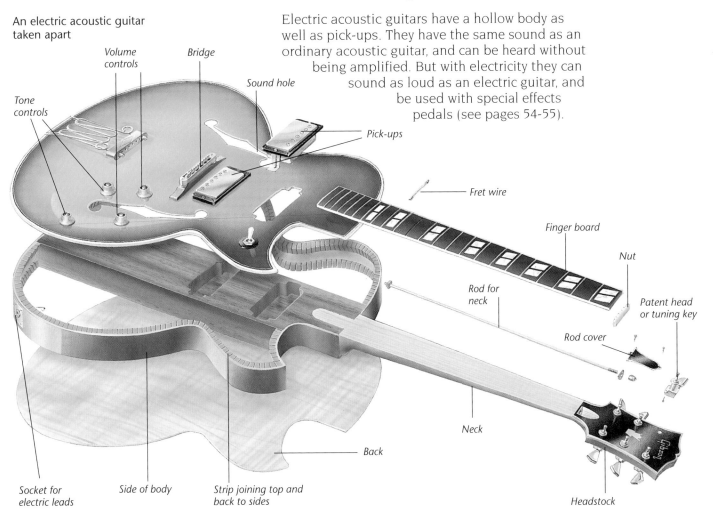

An electric acoustic guitar taken apart

Tone controls

Volume controls

Bridge

Sound hole

Pick-ups

Fret wire

Finger board

Nut

Rod for neck

Rod cover

Patent head or tuning key

Neck

Back

Socket for electric leads

Side of body

Strip joining top and back to sides

Headstock

Andantino (Küffner)

The word *simile* tells you to continue playing in the same way. In this tune it tells you to continue playing the melody-line notes with your right-hand fingers *a*, *m*, *i*, in that order.

This helps you to see quickly what fingers to use, and saves writing it out all the way through the piece. Play all the bass-line notes with your right-hand thumb.

Gibson ES345 electric acoustic (1967)

Sharps and flats

A sharp sign (♯) before a note makes it a fret higher. A flat sign (♭) makes it a fret lower.

These signs also affect any note later in the measure on the same line or space.

Sort of blue (Hooper)

Keep your second finger down on E in the first four measures, then on A for four measures.

The slanting line in the last measure tells you to move your finger up the neck to play the A.

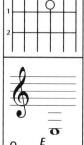

Chuck Berry, one of the finest rhythm-and-blues guitarists, playing a Gibson ES335 electric acoustic

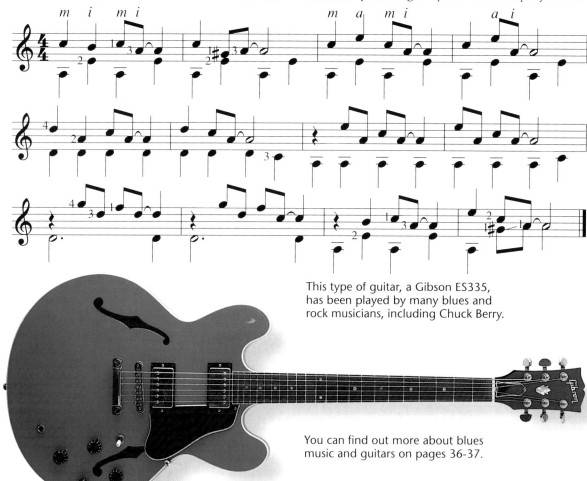

This type of guitar, a Gibson ES335, has been played by many blues and rock musicians, including Chuck Berry.

You can find out more about blues music and guitars on pages 36-37.

NEW NOTES

G♯

E

Allegro in C (Sor)

In this tune, damp the bass notes with your right thumb in the rests.

Lutes

Guitars are part of a large group of plucked stringed instruments called the lute family. Lutes were very popular in Europe from the late Middle Ages to the 18th century. They make a quiet but very clear sound. As well as being solo instruments, they were often used to accompany singers and other instruments. Lutes have a rounded back, and the sound hole, called a rose, is often decorated with ornate carving.

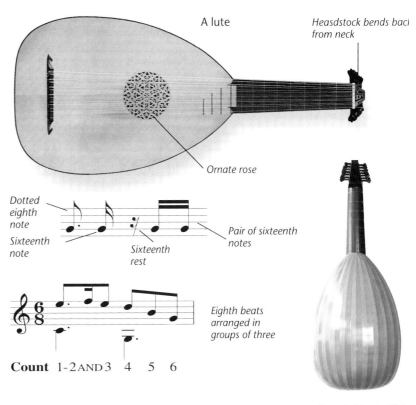

A lute

Heasdstock bends back from neck

Ornate rose

Sixteenth notes

A dotted eighth note is one and a half eighth notes. Half an eighth note is a sixteenth note.

Dotted eighth note

Sixteenth note

Sixteenth rest

Pair of sixteenth notes

6/8 time

In 6/8 time there are six eighth beats in a measure, in two groups of three. Count in eighth beats, or in dotted quarter beats, with two dotted quarter beats in a measure.

Eighth beats arranged in groups of three

Count 1-2 AND 3   4   5   6

Rounded back of lute made from strips of wood

Packington's pound

This tune was originally written for the lute.

Though famous as a classical guitarist, Julian Bream is also well-known as a lute player.

NEW NOTES

F♯

Key signatures

The sharp sign on the F line at the beginning of each staff below is called a key signature. It tells you to play all the Fs throughout the tune as F sharps.

D.C. *al Fine*

D.C. *al Fine* stands for *Da Capo al Fine*. It tells you to play the music again from the start. This time you stop playing when you reach the word *Fine*. *Fine* means "end".

Barcarolle (*Offenbach*)

This tune should sound very smooth and gentle.

Fine

D.C. al Fine

Jimi Hendrix, one of the most famous left-handed rock guitarists, used a right-handed Fender Stratocaster. He played it upside down, but did not restring it.

Left-handed guitars

Many left-handed guitarists hold and play the guitar as if they were right-handed. But some use their right hand for fingering and their left for playing, holding the guitar so it points to the right, not the left. The order of the strings is usually reversed so that the left-hand thumb still plays the lowest one. There are also specially made left-handed guitars, with the lowest string furthest to the right of the neck, and all the features reversed (see the Stratocaster on the right of page 19).

Right-handed Fender Stratocaster (1950s reissue) turned back to front, like the one Jimi Hendrix used

Upbeats

The next tune starts with a quarter beat before the first full measure. This is called an upbeat. Count three beats before you start.

The last measure of the tune only lasts for two beats. Together, the last measure and the upbeat make one complete measure.

Cockles and mussels

Left-handed Fender Stratocaster (1978)

Socket for jack-plug to amplifier

Tremolo arm to vary pitch of notes

Pick-up selector switch

Scratchplate to protect body

Button for strap

Three pick-ups

NEW NOTES

F#

Getting louder and quieter

The signs on the right tell you to get louder or quieter. To play louder, play the strings slightly harder, with your fingers more upright. Try not to change speed when you change volume.

Get louder. The word *crescendo* (or *cresc.*) can be used instead.

Get quieter. The word *diminuendo* (or *dim.*) can be used instead.

Minuet in G (Bach)

Wilkes Custom fretless bass

Bass guitars

Most bass guitars only have four strings. These are tuned to the same notes as the four lowest strings of an ordinary guitar, although they play lower versions of the notes. Most bands include a bass guitar, and use it along with the drums to give the music a solid rhythm. Some people also play the bass guitar successfully as a solo instrument.

Finger rest

Loud and quiet

The letters on the right tell you how loudly or quietly to play. They are called dynamics. Look for them in the music below.

p	(*piano*)	quiet
mp	(*mezzo piano*)	fairly quiet
f	(*forte*)	loud
mf	(*mezzo forte*)	fairly loud

Allegro (Giuliani)

Emphasize the bass line in this tune.

Stanley Clarke was one of the first electric bass players to use the instrument to play solos.

Microfrets bass (1970s)

Tuning keys are larger than on ordinary electrics

The Fender Precision bass was the first solid electric bass guitar to be made. It is still one of the most popular models today. The one shown here is a 1960s reissue.

Longer neck than ordinary electric

Thick steel-wound strings

String guide

21

PLAYING CHORDS

Chords are groups of two or more notes played at the same time. When chords are used for accompanying a tune, they are often shown by letter names above the staff, rather than written out as separate notes.

For example, the letter G above a tune tells you to play a G major chord. The photo on the left and the diagram on the right show you how to do this. Position your left-hand fingers, then play each string separately to check all the notes are sounding. Then run your thumb or plectrum across all the strings from the sixth to the first. This is called strumming.

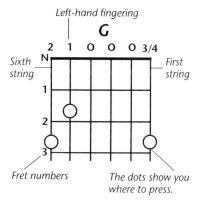

Left-hand fingering

G

Sixth string

First string

Fret numbers

The dots show you where to press.

Some chords sound better if you leave out some of the strings. For example, to play a C major chord you only strum the top five strings, and for a D major chord you play the top four strings.

C

A cross tells you not to play the string.

D

Try strumming the chords below (the chords have their names above the staff). Practice finding each chord shape slowly at first.

Then try changing from one to another. At first it may seem hard to remember where your fingers go, but it does become easier.

Pete Townshend, guitarist with the Who, played loud, aggressive chords by rotating his right arm from the shoulder, like a windmill.

Playing clear chords

If a note in a chord sounds dead, check to see if your finger is pressing hard enough, just behind the fret. Keep each left-hand finger upright. Your nails have to be fairly short.

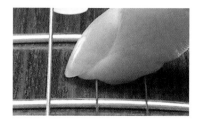

A long nail could stop you from keeping your fingers upright. This means you might touch another string.

Minor chords

Minor chords are another type of chord. In guitar music, the abbreviation "m" or "min" after the letter name tells you to play a minor chord.

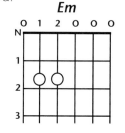

Em

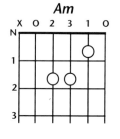

Am

Power chords

Power chords are bare-sounding two-note chords used in rock music. You can move the same shape up the neck to play different chords. They are named after the note you play with your left-hand first finger. In the music below, Roman numerals above the staff tell you at which fret to put your first finger*.

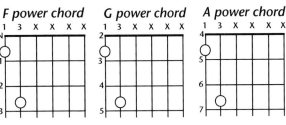

F power chord **G power chord** **A power chord**

For these power chords, only play the two lowest strings. Hit the strings firmly with a pick to get a full, biting sound.

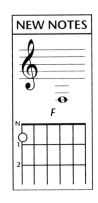

NEW NOTES

F

Full power

V I III

V I III

Bar chords

This chord shape is for F major.

Keep your first finger straight.

Keep your other fingers relaxed.

For some chords you have to put your first finger across all six strings. This is called a bar. Try making a bar at the fifth fret. Keep it straight, pressing firmly just behind the fret. Check that each string is sounding clearly. Then try making a bar at a lower fret. Playing with a bar can seem tricky at first, but it soon becomes easier.

F major is a very common bar chord. You can see how to play this below.

This shape has no open strings, so you can move it to any fret to play any major chord.

Kurt Cobain, guitarist with Nirvana, achieved a powerful, distorted sound by playing chords with a distortion pedal (see page 54 for more).

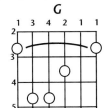

F

This curved line tells you to play a bar.

G

To change F major to F minor, you simply lift your second finger.

You can move the F minor shape up the finger board to play other minor chords.

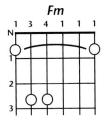

Fm

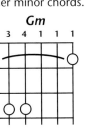

Gm

---

* I = 1st fret; III = 3rd fret; V = 5th fret, and so on.   23

PLAYING CHORDS WITH YOUR RIGHT HAND

You can use chords to accompany singers or other musicians. They can also sound very effective if you play them on their own.

To vary the way chords sound, there are many different ways of using your right hand. Below are some useful right-hand chord techniques.

Basic strum

With your thumb, first finger or a pick, strum a chord downward across the strings (from the lowest note to the highest) then back upward (back toward the lowest note). If you strum with your first finger, use the back of your fingernail to strum downward and your fingertip to strum upward.

Strum downward toward the highest note on the first beat.

Then strum upward, toward the lowest note.

Bass-chord strum

This strum is used a lot in country music (see page 37). You use your first finger or a pick.

The pictures below show you what to do. It is a variation of the basic strum.

First play the bass note of the chord with your thumb or with a pick.

Then strum the chord downward (toward the highest note) with your first finger or your pick.

You can add an extra upward strum if it fits the rhythm (see below for more about this).

Below are some rhythms to play for a bass-chord strum. In guitar music, arrows show you which way to strum. An up arrow means strum from the lowest note to the highest.

A down arrow means strum back toward the lowest note. This can be confusing, because an up arrow actually means strum downward and a down arrow means strum upward!

When there are two quarter beats in a measure, play the bass note on the first beat and strum once on the second beat.

You can vary the rhythm when there are two quarter beats in a measure by playing two fast eighth note strums on the second beat.

When there are three quarter beats in a measure, try two slow quarter note strums on the second and third beats of the measure.

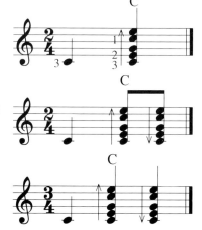
A selection of picks. The fourth one down is a thumb pick which is worn on the thumb. The fifth one is thicker and smaller and is used for playing jazz. The bottom one is called a shark fin pick.

Fingerpicking

Playing each note of a chord separately is called fingerpicking. Use your thumb for the bass note, and your first three fingers for the top three strings.

The music below shows you the rhythms and fingerings to use for fingerpicking chords. One is for 2/4 time, the other for 3/4.

Your third finger always plays the first string.

Your middle finger always plays the second string.

Your index finger always plays the third string.

Your thumb plays the bass note. This will be on the sixth, fifth or fourth string depending on the chord.

Alternate bass-chord picking

Alternate bass-chord picking is a variation of the bass-chord strum. This type of strum is also used a lot in country music. First play the bass note with your thumb or pick.

Then play the top three strings together with your fingers, or strum with a pick. Then play another bass note on a different string. Then play the rest of the chord again.

In the diagrams on the right, the solid dots indicate another bass note you can use.

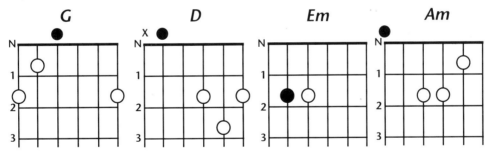

Chet Atkins, one of the best country-music guitarists, used elaborate fingerpicking patterns based on the ones shown on this page.

Below you can see the rhythms and notes to use for an alternate bass-chord strum on C.

The other bass note is the E which you normally play with your second finger.

For a three beat rhythm, play the bass note, then play or strum twice, then play a different bass note and repeat the two strums.

For a four beat rhythm, play the bass note then play or strum the chord once. Then play a different bass note, then play or strum again.

25

NEW NOTES

D♯

C♯

Repeat signs

A left repeat sign (with dots on the left) tells you to repeat the last section. Go back to the last right repeat sign, or, if there isn't one, go to the beginning and play the section again.

Left repeat sign

Right repeat sign

Emphasizing notes

A horizontal line above or below a note tells you to emphasize it slightly, so it sounds stronger than usual.

Prelude (Aguado)

Repeat the first eight measures of this tune, then play and repeat the next eight measures.

When you have figured out the notes, try to emphasize the notes marked with lines.

Washburn D325 acoustic

Naturals

A natural (♮) before a note affects any notes later in the measure on the same line or space.

It cancels out a sharp or flat in the key signature or earlier in the measure.

Amusement (Horetzky)

Triplets

Triplet eighth notes last for a third of a quarter beat. They are shown by a small 3 written just above or below the notes.

Spanish study

Try this tune slowly at first, remembering to play the first- and second-time measures.

First- and second-time measures

Some tunes with repeats have two different endings. The first time you play the music, play the measure marked 1 (first-time measure), then repeat. The second time, play the measure marked 2 (second-time measure) instead.

Count the beats carefully so you keep to a steady speed when you reach the triplets.

Gibson Chet Atkins acoustic (1989)

Birkett and Blackwell Custom acoustic

Top of pegs decorated with mother-of-pearl

Decorative edging strip around body

Pick guard

SCALES

A scale is a special sequence of notes. Most music is based on scales. There are many kinds and each one can start on any note.

One of the most common types of scale is the major scale. The scale of C major starts and ends on C.

C *major scale*

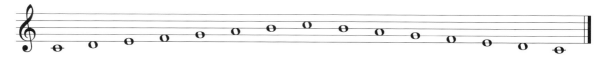

The step between two notes is called an interval. Major scales contain two kinds of interval: tones and semitones. On a guitar, there is a tone between any two notes that are two frets apart. There is a semitone between any two notes that are one fret apart.

In major scales, the tones and semitones always come in the same order: tone, tone, semitone, tone, tone, tone, semitone. The semitones in the C major scale are between E and F, and between B and C. These notes are a fret apart. The other notes are two frets apart.

Ovation Glen Campbell left-handed acoustic (detail of Ovation neck shown below)

The spots on the picture below show you where B and C and E and F are on the guitar. They are only one fret apart.

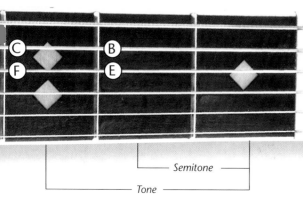

Robert Fripp, one of the most accomplished British guitarists, playing an Ovation acoustic

Try working out a major scale starting on G. The interval between each pair of notes is a tone (two frets) except for two semitones.

In a G major scale, the semitones are between B and C, and F sharp and G. These pairs of notes are only one fret apart.

G *major scale*

T = Tone; S = Semitone

Practicing scales will help you to become familiar with where notes are on the guitar.

When you no longer have to search for each note, tunes become much easier to play.

THE FIRST ELECTRIC GUITARS

In the 1920s and 1930s, it was often difficult to hear the guitar in a band, because it made a quieter sound than some of the other instruments. At around this time, guitar makers began to experiment with using pick-ups on acoustic guitars to make them louder.

The first true electric guitar was made by the Rickenbacker company in 1931. It became known as the Rickenbacker frying pan (shown on the right) because it has a long neck and small round body. It has a simple pick-up made from two large magnets.

The Gibson company made many early electric guitars. This one is an ES140, a model launched in 1950.

Rickenbacker frying pan

Strings are high above frets

Maple neck

Single pick-up

Since this time, electric guitars have been made in all shapes and sizes, ranging from traditional models to unusual and eye-catching designs.

Most modern versions have solid bodies. Two of the most popular and lasting designs are the Gibson Les Paul and the Fender Stratocaster.

The Fender Stratocaster was first produced in 1954. It has a light sound and is very popular with players of all types of rock music.

The Gibson Les Paul, first made in 1952, has a warm, full sound, and is popular with rock and blues players. Gibson developed it with a guitarist called Les Paul.

During the 1950s, Les Paul made several recordings with his wife, the singer Mary Ford, shown here.

Fender Stratocaster (1963)

Body color - Lake Placid Blue

Gibson Les Paul Custom (left-handed model)

Maple body

Body color - Cherry Sunburst

Pick-up surrounds strings

Connector for electric lead

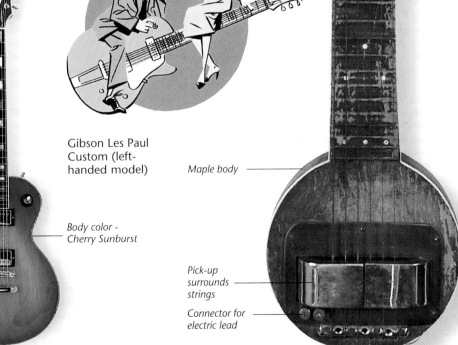

Playing in different positions

So far in this book your left hand has usually been positioned so that your first finger is at the first fret, your second finger at the second fret, and so on. This is called first position.

To play notes higher up the guitar, you have to move your hand so your first finger is at a higher fret. In second position your first finger is at the second fret, your second finger at the third fret, and so on. Roman numerals above the staff tell you what position to play in. For example, in *Sunset*, you start in second position (**II**), so you can reach the A in measure 2.

By changing hand position, you can often play a particular note on another string. This makes some combinations of notes easier to play.

The music below is a G major scale in second position. Follow the string numbers and fingerings very carefully.

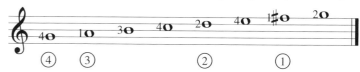

Spread chords

A wavy line before a chord tells you to play it as a spread chord. Play the notes quickly one after the other, not at the same time.

Speed words

The word *ritardando* (or *rit.*) tells you to slow down. After this, the words *a tempo* tell you to go back to your original speed.

Sunset (**Edge**)

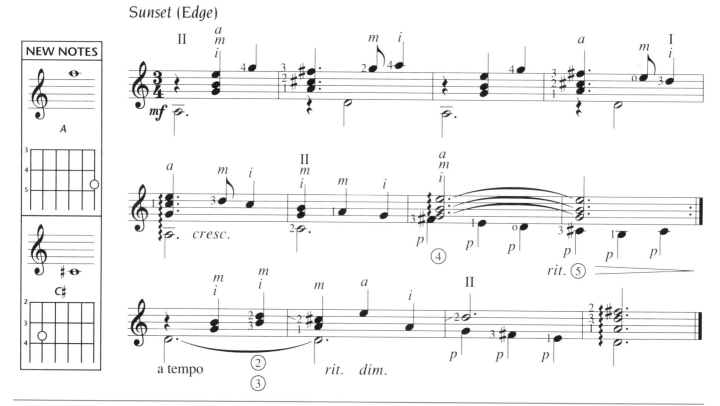

Letting notes ring

Sometimes instead of damping open strings at the end of the note, it sounds better to let them ring. A curved line after a note tells you to do this. You can see one after the A and the D in measures 13 and 14 of *Country air*.

Ring sign

Country air (Hooper)

Gretsch Tennessean electric acoustic (1960s), a popular guitar among country musicians

Country music

Country music developed in the southern USA in the early twentieth century. It is based on folk and traditional music. At first, people played it in their homes and at local concerts.

Later it became popular all over America through recordings and radio broadcasting. The guitar is one of the most important instruments in country music.

Gretsch electric acoustic guitars are very popular with country musicians. This model is a Double Anniversary (1964).

Eddie Cochran, a rock-and-roll singer and guitarist, began his career as a country musician. He often used Gretsch guitars.

Back and sides match dark green of pick guard

Two pick-ups

HAMMER-ON AND PULL-OFF

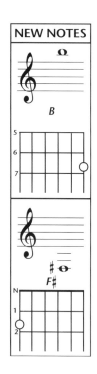

NEW NOTES

B

F#

In guitar music, a curved line linking different notes tells you to play smoothly. You finger all the notes, but only play the string once.

The techniques to do this are known as hammer-on and pull-off, or *ligado* (*ligar* is the Spanish word for "to bind" or "to tie").

Position your left hand so your second finger is ready to play at the second fret. Play your open D string with your right thumb.

Firmly hammer your left-hand second finger down on the string at the second fret. You will hear the note E.

Play the string again, then pull your second finger off sideways so it pulls the string. The open D will sound again.

Practice using these techniques with pairs of notes on each string. The string will continue to vibrate for a quite a while, so don't rush.

In the music on this double page, H above or below the curved line tells you to hammer a finger on and P tells you to pull it off.

Heavy hammer

Before you try playing this tune, practice your hammer-on and pull-off techniques in first position for a while to get a good sound.

Play this tune in fifth position (with your first finger at the fifth fret). The string numbers will help you find where the notes are.

Ibanez Mod.570 solid electric (often used for playing heavy metal music)

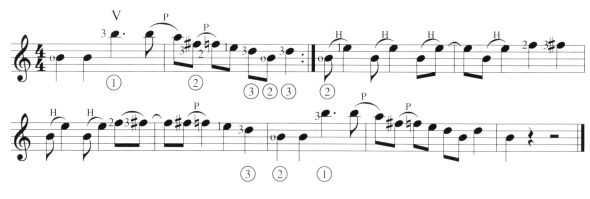

Up-country

Many country guitarists use hammer-on and pull-off techniques for chords.

Grace notes

A grace note is written as a small eighth note with a line through it just before a note. It is used to decorate the music. Play the string on the grace note, then hammer a finger on or pull it off to play the next note.

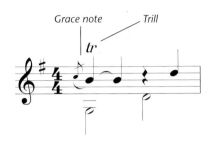

Trills

Trills are another kind of musical decoration. They use hammer-on and pull-off techniques to make two notes sound alternately several times. Try playing a simple trill using open G and A. First play a G, then hammer your second finger down on A and quickly pull it away again before the string stops vibrating. This means you hear three notes, but only play the string once. Try playing longer trills by hammering your finger down for a second time and pulling it off again. Trills are shown in music by *tr* written over a note. You play the note written in the music and the one above it.

The American heavy metal guitarist Eddie van Halen, playing a Kramer electric

Bourrée (Edge)

This tune contains four grace notes, each one followed by a note with *tr* written over it. At first learn the tune without playing the trills or grace notes. Then practice playing the grace notes, pulling your finger off to the next note. Then try adding in a trill as well, always making sure the rhythm stays steady.

Start with a simple trill (quickly hammer your finger on the note above, then pull it off). Then see if you can hammer your finger down and pull it off a second time before the string stops vibrating. With the grace note as well, that means you would hear six notes, but only play the string once.

Kramer Baretta solid electric, a popular heavy metal guitar

TWELVE-STRING GUITARS

On a twelve-string guitar, the strings are arranged in pairs. The strings in each pair are very close together, so you play both at once. In the top two pairs, both strings are tuned identically. In the other four pairs, one string is tuned as normal, while the extra string is tuned to the note an octave higher. Twelve-string guitars have a distinctive jangling sound. They are particularly popular for playing folk music, but some pop groups also use them.

George Harrison, guitarist with the Beatles, often played a Rickenbacker twelve-string.

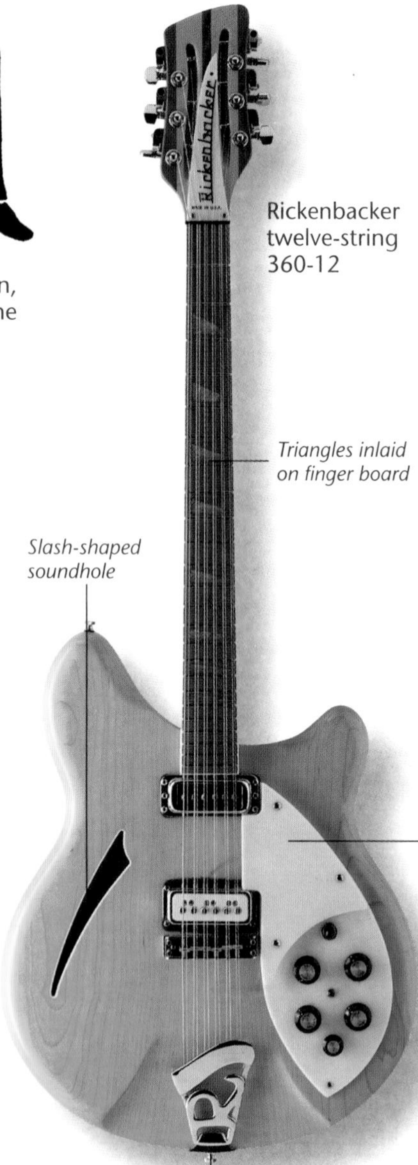

Fender Coronado twelve-string (1960s)

Pairs of strings strung consecutively on headstock

Rickenbacker twelve-string 360-12

Pair of strings

Triangles inlaid on finger board

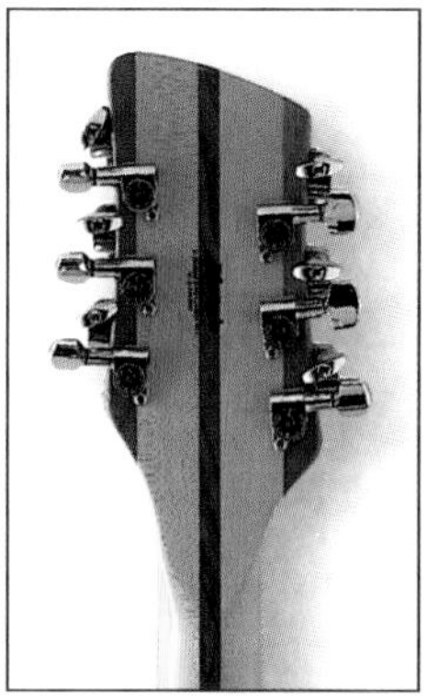

On a Rickenbacker twelve-string, the extra six tuning keys point backward instead of out to the side.

Slash-shaped soundhole

Vox Phantom twelve-string (1960s)

Split-level pick guard

Large "R" in tailpiece stands for Rickenbacker

"F" for Fender in tailpiece

USING A BAR

Sometimes, to reach all the notes, you need to press down more than one string at a time with your first finger. This is called using a bar. A full bar goes across six strings. If you press fewer than six strings, it is called a half bar.

This half bar covers four strings. Press firmly, right behind the fret.

The letter B means "full bar"; ½ B means "half bar". (For a half bar, use the music to work out which strings you need to press*.) The Roman numeral tells you at which fret to make the bar. The dotted line shows you how long to hold it.

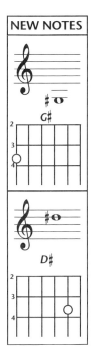

NEW NOTES

G#

D#

Dance (Giuliani)

Etude in D (Sor)

Ovation Adamas electric acoustic twelve-string (the black circles are sound holes)

BLUES GUITAR

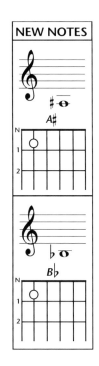
Blues music developed in America in the late 19th century. Early blues musicians played acoustic guitars to accompany themselves singing. Sometimes people played homemade instruments too. Today most blues bands use electric guitars.

Silvertone archtop acoustic (1950s), a popular jazz guitar

Lazy blues (*Edge*)

Bo Diddley, an American blues and rock singer, is famous for playing oddly shaped guitars.

Strumming the blues

The rhythms below are good to use for strumming chords to blues tunes.

String bending

String bending is often used by blues guitarists to add expression to the music.

Play a note, and as soon as it sounds, bend the string by pushing it with your left finger across the finger board. This alters the pitch.

In the music below, a curved arrow after a note shows you where to play a bend.

Bend the top three strings away from the edge of the neck towards the bottom strings.

Bend the bottom three strings sideways in the opposite direction, towards the first string.

The blues guitarist B.B. King calls his guitar Lucille.

Accents

A wedge-shaped sign above or below a note tells you to accent it. Play it more forcefully than usual.

Accent

Left-hand bend (**Edge**)

Very flat, solid body

The Fender Telecaster has a light, clear tone, and is very popular with blues musicians. This model is fitted with a "B-bender hipshot", a device that alters the pitch of the strings when the player hits it.

B-bender hipshot

MORE ABOUT PLAYING THE STRINGS

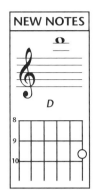

D

Rest stroke

A rest stroke is another way of playing the strings. It is useful for making notes sound louder. After you play the string, let your right-hand thumb or finger come to rest on the next string across instead of finishing in the air. In a tune you can use rest strokes to emphasize a melody line, or some of the bass notes.

After playing the third string with a rest stroke, your finger should come to rest on the fourth string.

Your thumb would come to rest on the third string after a rest stroke on the fourth string.

Ocean blue (Edge)

In this tune, play all the melody-line notes with rest strokes. This will make them sound emphasized. Remember to follow all the other instructions in the music as well.

Start getting slower in measure 8, then go back to your original speed in measure 10. After the D.C. *al Fine*, go to the beginning and play the music again up to the *Fine* sign.

Chrissie Hynde, guitarist and lead singer with the Pretenders, playing a Gibson Les Paul

38

Playing with *vibrato*

Try playing a note and rocking your left hand quickly from side to side. The pitch of the note gets slightly higher and lower. This effect is called *vibrato*. Try playing *Ocean blue* again, adding some *vibrato* on the melody notes. Try it in some of the other pieces in this book too.

Rock your hand from side to side.

Frank Zappa playing a Gibson SG like the one shown below

Damping strings

String damping makes the music sound very rhythmic and percussive. Touch the strings with the edge of your hand while you play.

In the music at the bottom of the page, the sign ∧ above a chord tells you when to damp the strings.

Touch the strings lightly, right over the bridge. The sound should not be completely dead.

If you touch the strings too far in front of the bridge, you will damp them too much.

You can also damp the strings after playing a note with the side of your hand and thumb.

Damper than damp

String damping is often used in reggae, a style which originated in Jamaica in the 1960s. Many reggae songs have an unusual guitar rhythm, which is created by playing accented chords with damped strings on the second and fourth beats of each measure.

Try the chords below, damping the strings. You could also try using other rhythms with damped chords. For example, try playing damped eighth notes or quarter notes on the second and fourth beats of the measure, and insert an undamped chord on the third beat.

Gibson SG electric

39

EARLY GUITARS

The history of the guitar in Europe goes back to the 15th century. Up until this time, most plucked stringed instruments were based on the lute (see page 17). The earliest surviving guitars date from the 16th century, and are much smaller than guitars used today.

The strings were tuned in sets of one or two strings called courses. The earliest guitars had four courses. From the late 15th century, five-course guitars became popular, especially in Italy. Six-course guitars were made in the 17th and 18th centuries.

A five-course guitar, made by René Verboam in 1641

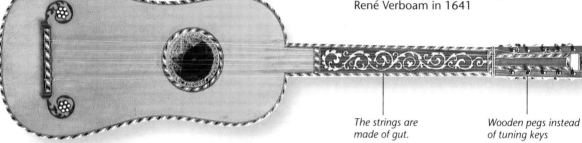

The strings are made of gut.

Wooden pegs instead of tuning keys

A five-course guitar made in the 1680s by Antonio Stradivari. Stradivari was best known as a violin maker.

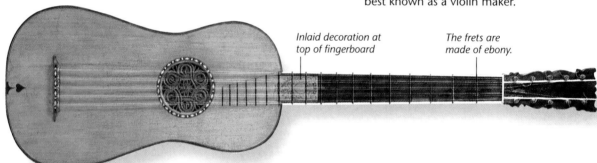

Inlaid decoration at top of fingerboard

The frets are made of ebony.

The chitarra battente was a type of guitar made during the 17th and 18th centuries. It was mainly used to accompany popular music. It had a curved back and was probably played with a pick.

The strings are fixed to the bottom of the body.

A chitarra battente, made in 1627 by Giorgio Sellas

The strings and frets are made of metal.

Mistris Winters jumpe (Dowland)

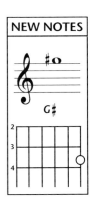

NEW NOTES

G#

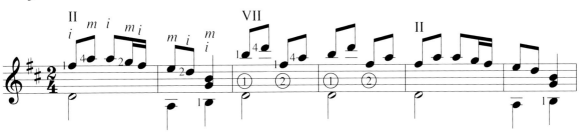

A toy

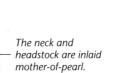

Göran Söllscher, a guitarist famous for playing early lute and guitar music on early instruments

The neck and headstock are inlaid mother-of-pearl.

The body is decorated with inlaid ivory and ebony.

The pieces on this page were both written in the 16th century.

THE DEVELOPMENT OF THE GUITAR

NEW NOTES

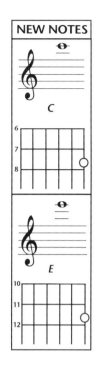

C

E

In the 17th and 18th centuries, guitars were often made with six courses instead of five. Guitars with six single strings were introduced in the 18th century. By the late 19th century, six single strings had become standard.

Tuning keys had replaced wooden pegs. Most guitars had flat backs, and metal frets. A Spanish guitar maker, Antonio de Torres Jurado (1817-92), established the standard size and design for the modern classical guitar.

A 17th-century six-course guitar, made in Lisbon, Portugal, by Santos Vieyra

Ivory pegs

Wood and ivory inlay on neck

Romanza

Andrés Segovia was reponsible for making classical guitar widely popular in the early part of this century.

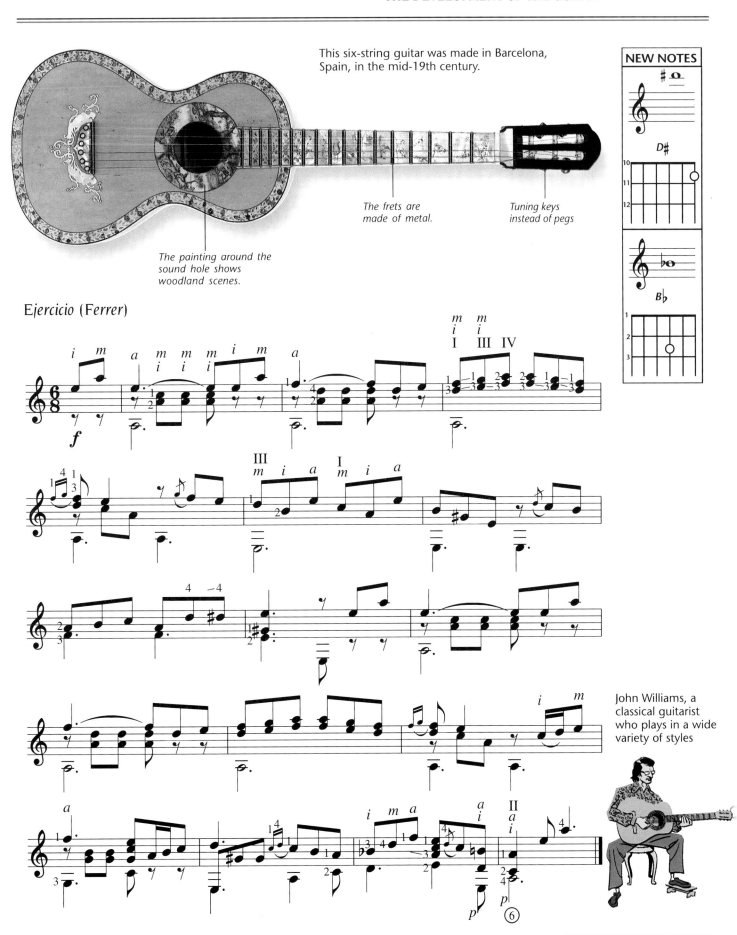

This six-string guitar was made in Barcelona, Spain, in the mid-19th century.

The frets are made of metal.

Tuning keys instead of pegs

The painting around the sound hole shows woodland scenes.

NEW NOTES

D#

Bb

Ejercicio (Ferrer)

John Williams, a classical guitarist who plays in a wide variety of styles

PLAYING HARMONICS

Harmonics are bell-like notes made by gently touching a string instead of pressing it down. You can only play harmonics at certain frets.

Try playing a harmonic at the twelfth fret on the sixth string with your third or fourth finger (this fret may be marked with a dot).

The Edge, guitarist with U2, achieves a distinctive "ringing" sound by combining electronic effects (see pages 54-55) and harmonics.

Gently touch the string, right over the fret. Do not press down.

Play the string with your right-hand thumb or a finger.

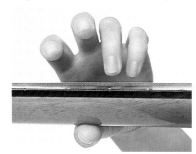

Quickly lift your left-hand finger off the string to let the note ring.

A harmonic is written as a diamond-shaped note at the pitch of the string on which you play it. It has "arm." and a number above it.

The number tells you which fret to play at. There are harmonics at the 4th, 5th, 7th, 9th and 12th frets.

D.C. *al Coda*

D.C. *al Coda* means repeat from the start to the instruction "To Coda". Then go to the section marked *Coda* and play to the end.

Staccato

A dot above or below a note tells you to make it very short. Damp the string with your right-hand thumb or finger after you play it.

Clockwise (Edge)

Play strictly in time until the *Coda*. *Più lento* means "more slowly".

As guitarist with the Jam, Paul Weller often used a Rickenbacker electric. Later he also became known for his acoustic playing.

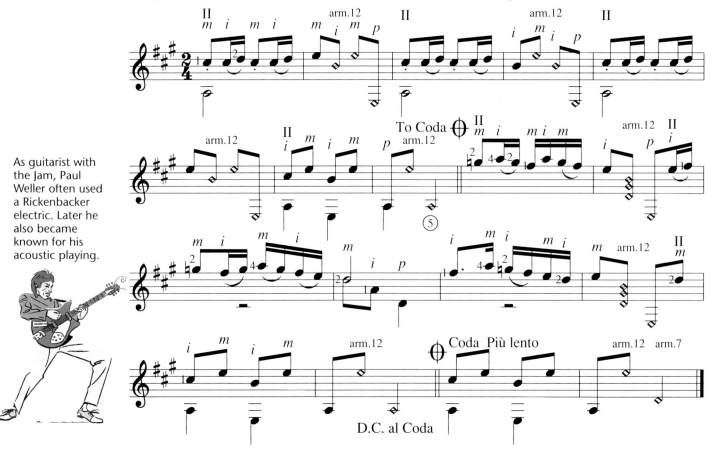

44

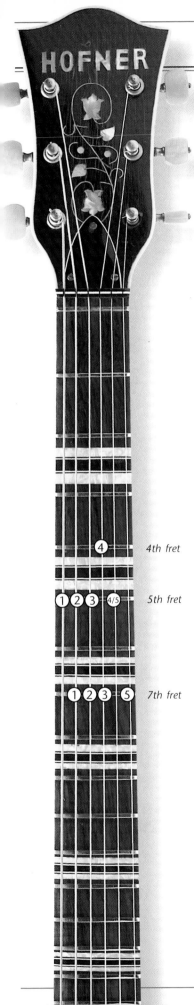

Practicing harmonics

Harmonics can be tricky at first. Remember to lift your left-hand finger as soon as you have played the string.

Also, try laying your third or fourth finger over all the strings to play six harmonics at once.

Tuning using harmonics

Tuning your guitar using harmonics is one of the most accurate methods. This is because harmonic notes make a very clear, pure sound. First tune your sixth string using a pitch pipe, tuning fork, electronic tuner or keyboard (see page 5).

4th fret

Play a harmonic at the fifth fret on the sixth string. Then quickly play a harmonic at the seventh fret on the fifth string, so you hear both notes at once. Tune your fifth string so the harmonics are exactly the same.

5th fret

7th fret

Using harmonics, tune each string to the one below it, as shown in the picture on the left. The numbered dots show you which pairs of harmonics should sound identical, and the order in which to tune the pairs. Always start from the sixth string and work up, one string at a time.

Lastly, play a harmonic at the twelfth fret on the first string against one at the fifth fret on the sixth string. If your guitar is in tune, they will sound exactly an octave apart.

Hofner Violin guitar (1960s)

A Hofner Verithin electric acoustic from the 1960s (detail of neck shown on the left)

Instead of the usual dots, inlaid stripes of mother-of-pearl mark the 3rd, 5th, 7th, 9th, 12th and 15th frets.

Waltz (Ferrer)

The lute (see page 17) is an early relative of the guitar.

Relatives of the guitar

The guitar has many relatives in the lute family which have been played in different parts of the world for hundreds of years.

Banjos have a body made from a piece of skin or plastic stretched over a metal frame. They usually have a wooden back to make the sound louder. Some banjos have an extra string for playing melodies, called the thumb string.

The cuatro is a type of guitar from Venezuela. It has four strings.

The sitar is a type of lute played in India since the 11th century. The type used today developed in the 18th and 19th centuries. It has seven main strings which are plucked with a pick.

Peg for thumb string

Tension screws on the frame adjust the tightness of the skin.

Metal frame

Skin or plastic body

The bridge is held onto the body by the strings.

"Sympathetic" strings vibrate when the main ones are played.

Andante in A minor (Carulli)

At the end of this piece, go back to the 𝄋 sign and continue to the *Fine*.

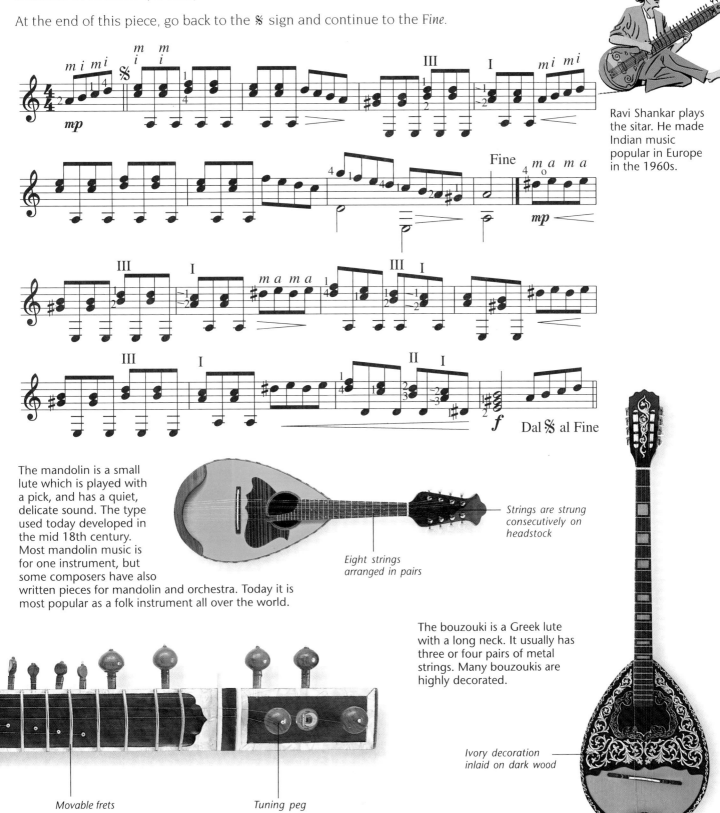

Ravi Shankar plays the sitar. He made Indian music popular in Europe in the 1960s.

The mandolin is a small lute which is played with a pick, and has a quiet, delicate sound. The type used today developed in the mid 18th century. Most mandolin music is for one instrument, but some composers have also written pieces for mandolin and orchestra. Today it is most popular as a folk instrument all over the world.

Strings are strung consecutively on headstock

Eight strings arranged in pairs

The bouzouki is a Greek lute with a long neck. It usually has three or four pairs of metal strings. Many bouzoukis are highly decorated.

Ivory decoration inlaid on dark wood

Movable frets

Tuning peg

FLAMENCO GUITAR

Flamenco is an expressive and dramatic style of music and dance from Andalusia in southern Spain. Originally, guitars were used in flamenco to accompany a singer, but now have their own solo style. The music is very rhythmic, and guitarists often tap the body of the guitar as they play, to get a percussive effect. Flamenco players have long right-hand finger nails for plucking the strings.

Paco de Lucia, one of the most famous flamenco guitarists

Plastic fingerplates protect the body when it is tapped.

Rasguado

Rasguado is a Spanish word which means "strum". It refers to a special technique used in flamenco playing. The pictures below show you what to do.

Sabicas was one of the first guitarists to make flamenco popular outside Spain.

Place your right hand just behind the sound hole with your fingers curled under.

Uncurl the three fingers *a*, *m* and *i* in that order so they strum across the strings.

Make each finger take over smoothly from the last until all your fingers have uncurled.

In music, a wavy arrow before a chord, or the term "*rasg*", tells you to play with a *rasguado* strum. A *rasguado* sounds very effective if you damp the strings right away.

When your fingers have uncurled, your hand should be held out flat over the strings. You can place it palm down over all six strings to stop them from vibrating.

Dotted measure lines

In the next tune, the measure with the *Fine* sign in it has a dotted measure line before the last note. This is because the tune starts on an upbeat. After the D.C. *al Fine*, go to the beginning of the tune as usual and play to the *Fine* sign. You stop at the dotted measure line, before the last note in the measure.

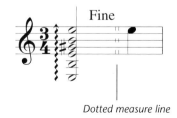

Dotted measure line

Flamenco guitars look similar to classical guitars, but are usually made of much lighter wood, such as cypress. Plastic fingerplates protect the body when the player taps it.

The strings on flamenco guitars are usually close to the finger board and have a high tension (see page 60). This helps the player to make a strong, percussive sound.

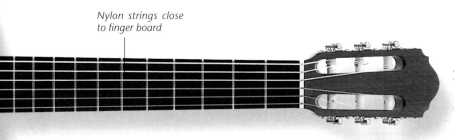

Nylon strings close to finger board

A Condé Hermanos flamenco guitar made in Madrid (Spain) in 1989

A flamenco dancer

Flim-flam flamenco (Edge)

The piece below is in a flamenco style using some *rasguado* strums. After you reach the D.C. al Fine, play the first section again once.

Then play the second-time measure, and repeat the second section to the *Fine* as often as you like, getting faster.

The guitarist Paco Peña runs his own group of flamenco dancers and musicians.

JAZZ GUITAR

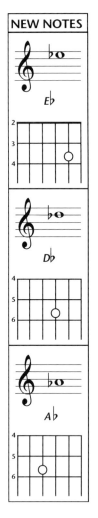

NEW NOTES

Eb

Db

Ab

Jazz began in the early 1900s in America. It combines different ideas from European, American and African styles of music.

Jazz musicians use distinctive chords and compose tunes over them as they play. This is called improvising.

Clouds (Edge)

This tune contains lots of jazz chords. The ones in measures six and seven all use the same bar shape. Figure this out carefully.

The chords in measures eight, nine and ten all use another bar shape. Practice the chords before you try playing the whole piece.

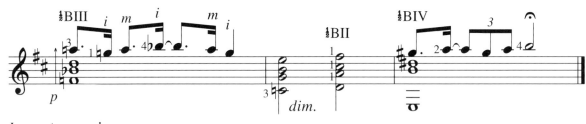

Charlie Christian was one of the first jazz players to use an electric guitar.

Jazz strumming

The rhythms below are good for strumming chords to accompany jazz tunes or songs.

Try damping some of the chords for a different effect.

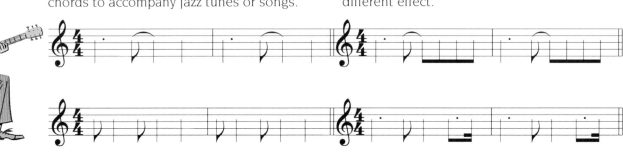

Shaggy rag (Hooper)

This tune is in a style called ragtime, which is closely related to jazz. It was very popular from the late 19th century until the 1920s.

Watch for the tied rhythms and the grace notes as you play. Count carefully, making sure you keep to a steady beat.

John McLaughlin, a British jazz and rock guitarist, playing a Gibson twin-neck guitar

Many jazz guitarists prefer electric acoustic instruments because they are capable of making many different types of guitar sounds.

An electric acoustic can sound mellow and gentle like an ordinary acoustic, or powerful and sustained like a solid instrument.

A Bigsby tremolo arm lets the player alter the pitch of the strings.

Pick-up selector switch enables player to change sounds quickly

Most electric acoustics have distinctive f-shaped sound holes.

Epiphone Sorrento electric acoustic (1965)

Gibson L5CES Custom electric acoustic (1978)

Tanglewood L5 Jazz model electric acoustic

Gibson ES175cc electric acoustic (1978)

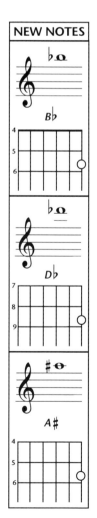

NEW NOTES

B♭

D♭

A♯

SLIDE GUITAR

Slide guitar technique originated in Hawaii. It involves sliding from one note to another, instead of playing them separately. Originally slide guitarists held their instruments in their laps. They used the necks of bottles to cover the strings and then slid them along the neck.

Today, slide guitar (often called bottleneck guitar) is usually played in a normal standing or sitting position. Instead of using a bottle, there are special slides made of metal, glass or ceramic. Each type of slide gives a slightly different sound.

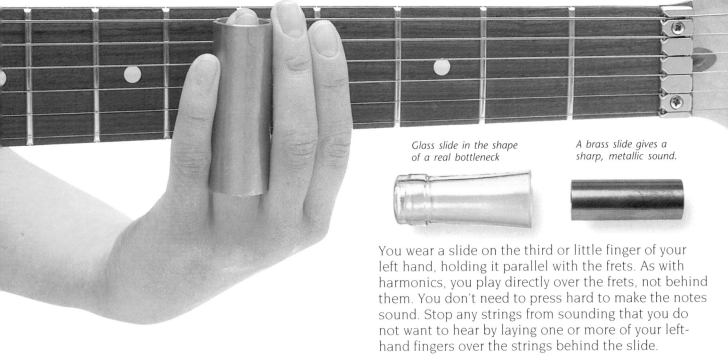

Glass slide in the shape of a real bottleneck

A brass slide gives a sharp, metallic sound.

You wear a slide on the third or little finger of your left hand, holding it parallel with the frets. As with harmonics, you play directly over the frets, not behind them. You don't need to press hard to make the notes sound. Stop any strings from sounding that you do not want to hear by laying one or more of your left-hand fingers over the strings behind the slide.

Open tunings

Dobro resonator guitar (1930s) made of metal, popular with many blues and slide guitarists (detail of neck shown right)

A slide sounds effective if you tune your open strings to play a major chord. This is called an open tuning, and will produce a major chord at whatever fret you place the slide. Some players tune to A, G and E chords, but these involve tightening the strings, and can put a lot of strain on the neck of the guitar, especially if it is a classical instrument.

Another common open tuning is D, with the strings tuned to a chord of D major - from the bottom up, D, A, D, F#, A and D. (You do not need to change the fourth and fifth strings.) First of all, tune the sixth string down a little, so that it plays the note D an octave below the fourth string. Then follow the numbered instructions on the picture below.

① *On the fourth string, play an F sharp at the fourth fret. Tune the third string down to match this.*

② *On the third string, play an A at the third fret. Tune the second string down to this note.*

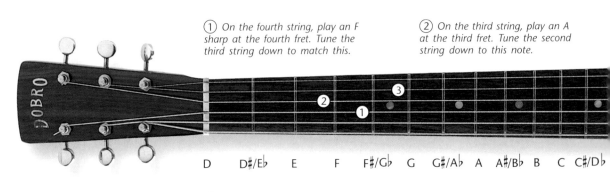

D   D#/E♭   E   F   F#/G♭   G   G#/A♭   A   A#/B♭   B   C   C#/D♭

③ *On the second string, play a D at the fifth fret. Tune the first string down to this note.*

The letters below the neck show the chords you can play at each fret using a slide over all six strings.

Slide time (Edge)

Play this piece with your strings tuned to a D chord (see last page). It will sound best on a steel-string acoustic or an electric guitar. The slanting lines in the music show you where you have to slide along the guitar neck. Play the string on the first note of the slide.

Then move your left hand to make the slide sound. Don't play the string again on the next note. The notes in parenthesis give you an idea of where you could start to slide from. There are fret numbers above the staff and string numbers below to help you

Son House, a blues guitarist, often played an open-tuned Dobro with a slide.

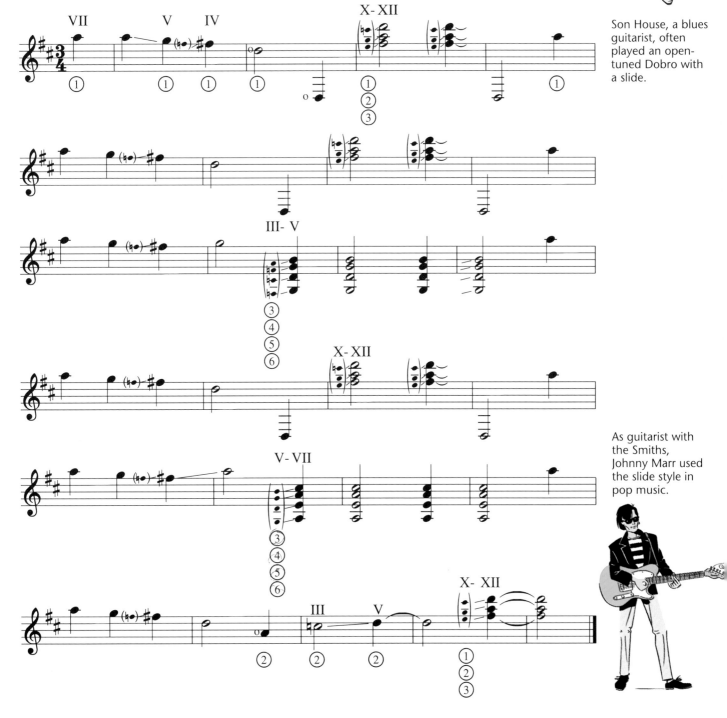

As guitarist with the Smiths, Johnny Marr used the slide style in pop music.

Bass rock (Edge)

If you have an electric guitar you could try playing this piece with a distortion pedal.

You can find out more about this below. The tune continues on the opposite page.

Gibson Flying V
solid electric

Guitar effects

Many electric guitarists use effects units to alter the sound of their instruments. These are usually plugged in between the guitar and amplifier. They change the guitar sound by altering the signal from the pick-ups.

Most units have a footswitch to turn the effect on and off. There may also be other controls to vary the level or speed of the effect. On some units, the harder the pedal is pressed, the more intense the effect.

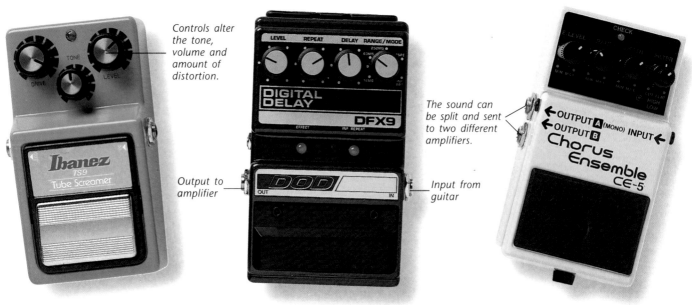

A distortion pedal. Distortion is a common guitar effect. It can make the sound fuzzy and muffled, or loud and piercing.

Controls alter the tone, volume and amount of distortion.

A delay unit. This repeats the signal, giving an echo effect. The number of repeats, and the gap between them, can be altered.

The sound can be split and sent to two different amplifiers.

Output to amplifier

Input from guitar

A chorus unit. Chorus makes the sound smooth, and can create the effect of several guitars playing together.

When you reach the end of the second line of music on this page, go back to the 𝄋 sign.

Continue to the first *Coda* sign, then play the section marked *Coda* to finish the piece.

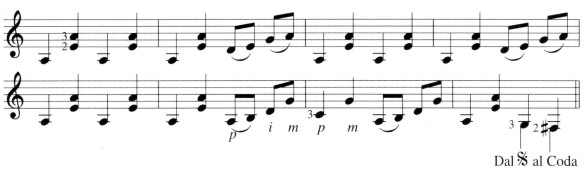

Dal 𝄋 al Coda

arm.12

Coda

♮BIII ♮BII

Fender Jaguar electric (1965)

The wahwah pedal creates a "wailing" sound by alternately boosting and cutting the treble and bass.

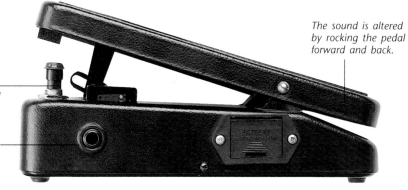

The sound is altered by rocking the pedal forward and back.

On/off switch operated by pedal

Output to amplifier

This multi-effects unit has several different effects built into one box. You can select which ones to use by pressing the different switches.

Different combinations of effects can be selected and displayed here.

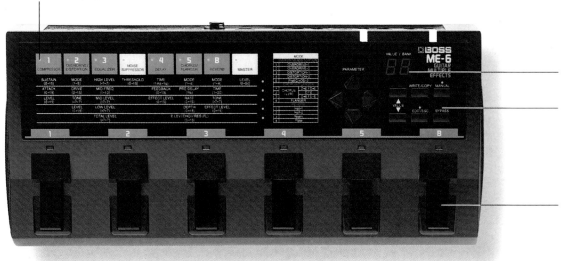

Digital display shows which combination of effects has been selected

Combinations can be stored in the memory and used at a later date.

Single effects or combinations of effects can be selected using the foot pedals.

The next four tunes are to play with other people. Each person plays the same staff in each group of two or three throughout a tune.

Before you play with a friend, both learn your own parts carefully. Count a few measures out loud before you start. Don't stop if you play wrong.

Cool cat (**Edge**)

Supro electric (1960s) made of resoglass (a type of fibreglass)

Danelectro electric (1950s)

D.C. al Fine

Ballad (*Edge*)

Burns Duo Sonic electric (1960s)

Gibson Les Paul Recording (1970s)

Greensleeves

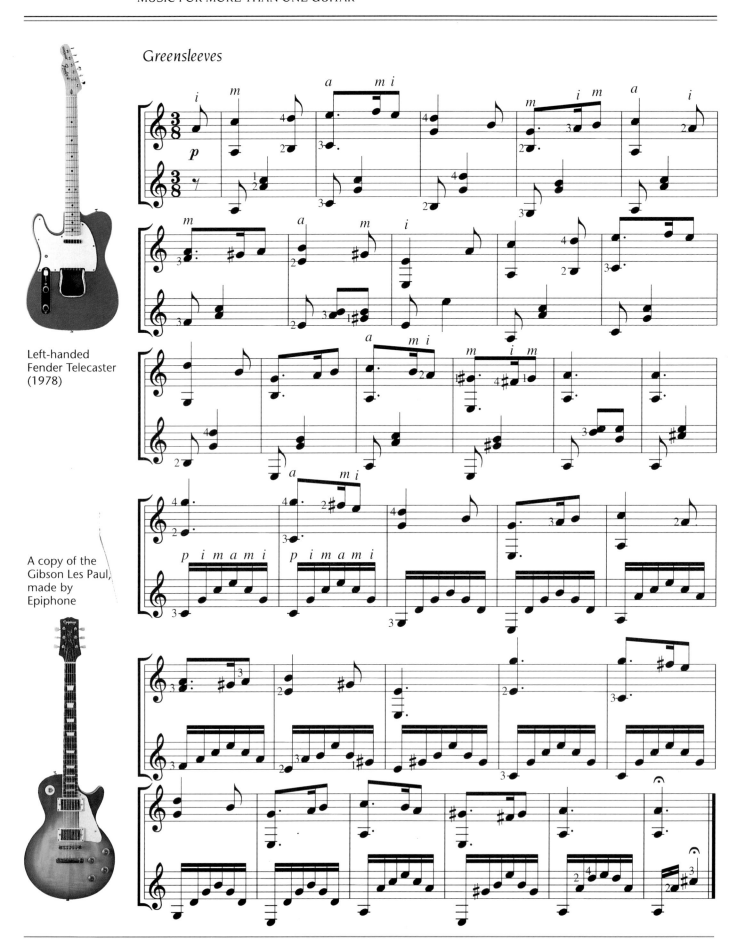

Left-handed
Fender Telecaster
(1978)

A copy of the
Gibson Les Paul,
made by
Epiphone

Rocking song (Edge)

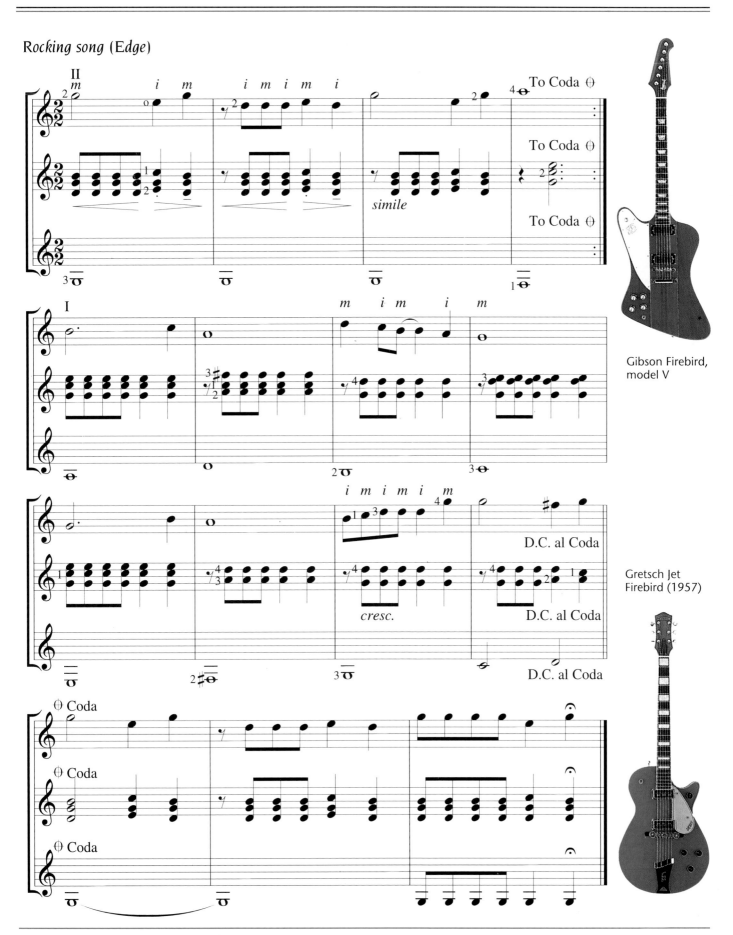

Gibson Firebird,
model V

Gretsch Jet
Firebird (1957)

In this tune, one person can play the bottom two staves in each group.

59

BUYING A GUITAR

Before you buy a guitar, try out several. Remember that sound is more important than appearance. Some shops will let you take a couple of guitars home for a few days to try out. This can help you decide. Below are some other things to look for.

1. Check that all the parts are securely fastened to the body, and that the neck is supported by a heel. If you want an acoustic guitar, make sure the soundboard is made of solid wood, not plywood. This gives the guitar a better sound.

2. Check that you can press the strings down easily all along the neck. If the strings are too high above the fingerboard they will be hard to press down. If they are too close to the fingerboard they may buzz when you play. You can have the height of the strings (called the action) altered (set) by a repairman.

High action classical guitar neck

Low action electric guitar neck

3. Hold the guitar up to eye level. Close one eye, and look down the length of the neck towards the body (the gaps between the frets should be only just visible). Check that all the frets are parallel.

4. Compare the pitch of the 12th fret harmonic of any string to the same note at the 12th fret. If they are not identical, but the action is set correctly, you may need a guitar repairman to adjust the saddle or nut. This is difficult on a classical or acoustic guitar, but much simpler on an electric guitar.

5. Play some notes on all the strings, all along the fingerboard. Think about whether you like the sound, how comfortable the guitar feels, and whether it stays in tune well.

6. If you want an electric guitar, check the sound when it is plugged into an amplifier. Check the pick-ups and control workings.

Buying new strings

The strings on a guitar gradually stretch as you play. Eventually they sound dull and become hard to tune. Sometimes they break too. When you replace a string, make sure it is the same type as the other strings you are using.

Bead

Steel strings are for electric guitars and steel-string acoustics. They are sold by their gauge (thickness). Gauges range from heavy to extra light. Light strings are the easiest to press, but can be hard to keep in tune, and are not as loud as thicker strings. Never use steel strings on a classical guitar or you will damage the neck.

Nylon strings are used on classical guitars. They come in different tensions, medium, high and very high. Medium are often the easiest type to use, but flamenco and some other styles sound better with high tension strings.

CHANGING STRINGS

When you change a string, always start by loosening the old one gently from the tuning key. This means you do not alter the tension on the neck too suddenly. When you tighten the new one up, keep your face well away in case the string breaks and lashes out. Never tighten it more than a tone above its correct pitch.

This may make it break and could bend the neck of the guitar. New strings always stretch a lot at first, so you have to keep retuning them while you are playing. Strings are fitted differently on different types of guitar. The pictures below show you how to restring each type.

Changing a nylon string

1. Loosen the old string at the tuning key and untie it at the bridge. Push about 6cm (2½in) of the new string down through the bridge toward the bottom of the guitar.

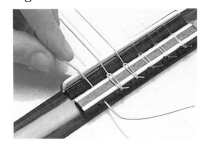

2. Bring the end back over the bridge and loop it under the rest of the string. Then bring it back down over the bridge, pushing it under itself.

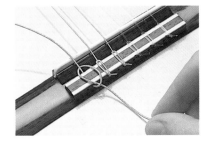

3. You can thread the string over and under itself once more on the bridge to make a more secure knot. Cut off the end of the string so that it doesn't rattle against the body.

4. Push the other end of the string through the hole in the tuning key leaving about 5cm (2in) slack. Tuck the loose end in.

5. Turn the tuning key to wind the string neatly in a coil. Coil the string toward the center of the headstock. Check that the string is in its grooves on the nut and saddle.

Changing a steel string

1. Loosen the old string at the tuning key, then release it from the bridge. Often you do this by pulling out a pin. Then put the bead of the new string into the hole, and push the pin back in.

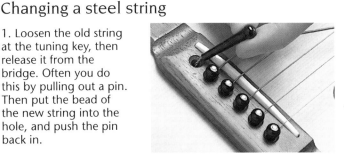

2. Electric acoustic guitars often have a tailpiece with a hole for each string. Loosen the old string, thread it out, and replace it with the new one.

3. The strings on solid body electric guitars sometimes go right through the body. Loosen the old string, pull it out from the back, then thread the new one through to the front.

4. Pull the string up to the tuning key. Thread the string through the hole in the capstan (the metal post), out toward the edge of the guitar. Leave about 5cm (2in) of string slack.

5. Start tightening the string. As you turn the tuning key, coil the string neatly around the capstan, toward the headstock. Coil the loose end around or snip it off.

How to play the notes in this book

Below you can check how to play all the notes used in the tunes in this book. For a note which you can play in first position (with your first finger at the first fret), a number in front of it tells you which finger to press.

For notes which you cannot play in first position, a Roman numeral above the staff tells you at which fret to press. A circled number below each note tells you which string to play.

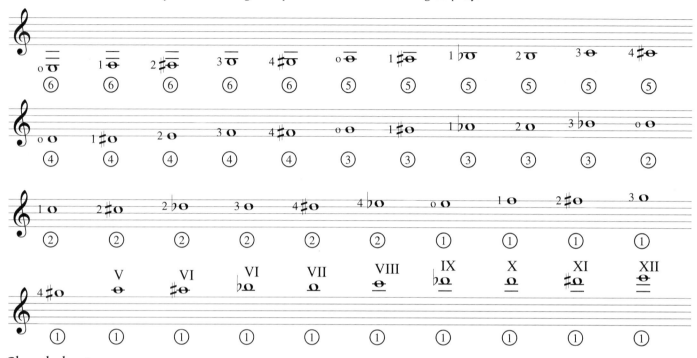

Chord chart

This chart shows you how to play some of the most common chords. The vertical lines represent the strings (with the sixth string furthest on the left). The horizontal lines show the frets, with fret numbers next to them. Dots show you where to press your fingers.

Finger numbers are shown above the strings. A zero tells you to play an open string; a cross tells you not to play the string. A curved line going across the diagram tells you to play with a bar (with your first finger pressed across the strings shown by the line).

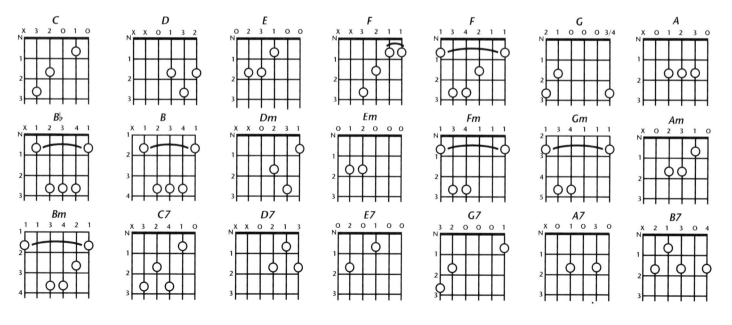

Tips on playing the pieces

In general, when you are learning a piece, practice any difficult parts slowly at first, until you can play them. The fingering suggestions in the music should make the notes easier to play, but if you find you cannot reach all the notes easily with your left hand, try figuring out your own fingering instead.

Minute minuet (page 10): Use your left-hand fourth finger to play D and G in this tune, as shown in the fingering. This will help you to reach the other notes more easily and comfortably.

Moderato (page 11): *Moderato* means "at a moderate speed", not too fast or too slow.

Andantino (page 11): *Andantino* means "a little faster than walking pace".

Allegretto (page14): *Allegretto* means "fairly lively".

Allegro in C (page 16): *Allegro* means "fast and lively". *Simile* tells you to continue playing *m i m i* with your right hand.

Packington's pound (page 17): This tune is a lot easier than it looks!

Barcarolle (page 18): A barcarolle has a lilting rhythm.

Minuet in G (page 20): A minuet is an elegant French dance with three beats in a measure. Use your first finger at the second fret where shown to help you reach the notes easily.

Bourrée (page 33): A *bourrée* is a fairly fast French dance.

Lazy blues (page 36): Watch for the slurs which tell you to hammer a finger on or pull it off. Take care not to confuse them with the ties (for example in measure 2).

Damper than damp (page 39): Strum this piece with a pick. Count carefully and make sure you keep to a steady beat.

Romanza (page 42): Use rest stroke for the first melody note in each triplet, trying to make them sound very smooth. Practice measures 9 and 10 until all the notes sound clearly.

Clockwise (page 44): All the harmonics in this piece are at the 12th fret, except for the last one, which is at the 7th fret.

Waltz (page 46): A waltz is a dance with three beats in a measure which is faster than a minuet. In measures 3 and 4, move your left-hand first finger smoothly.

Andante (page 47): *Andante* means "at a walking pace".

Tablature

Tablature is another way of writing down guitar music, often used for lute music and rock guitar. It uses sets of six lines, each one representing a string. Numbers on the lines tell you at which fret to play. On the right you can see a few notes written in ordinary notation with the same thing in tablature below.

Index of tunes

INDEX

Acknowledgements

The publishers are grateful to Andy's Guitar Workshop, Denmark Street, London, who provided over 50 of the guitars photographed for this book.

The publishers would also like to thank the following for the use of photographic and other material:
    Ashmolean Museum, Oxford (pages 40-41, page 42)
    Victoria & Albert Museum, London (page 43)
    Rickenbacker International Corporation, California, USA (page 29, right)
    Stephen Gottlieb (lute maker), London (page 17, page 46, top left)
    Macari's, London (page 54, bottom)

The models in the photographs were Charles Haworth, Fiona Watt and Harriet Castor.

First published in 1994 by Usborne Publishing Ltd, Usborne House, 83-85 Saffron Hill, London EC1N 8RT. First published in America March 1995.

Printed in Portugal. AE

3 1502 00446 1016